DAILY WISDOM
Vibes Unveiled
A groovy tarot guide to finding cool vibes

Amanda M Clarke

Copyright © 2024 by Koru Lifestylist

All rights reserved. All content, materials, and intellectual property in this book or any other platform owned by Koru Lifestylist are protected by copyright laws. This includes text, images, graphics, videos, audio, software, and any other form of content that may be produced by Koru Lifestylist.

No part of this content may be reproduced, distributed, or transmitted in any form or by any means without the prior written permission of Koru Lifestylist. This means that you cannot copy, reproduce, or use any of the content in this book for commercial or personal purposes without the express written consent of Koru Lifestylist.

Unauthorized use of any copyrighted material owned by Koru Lifestylist may result in legal action being taken against you. Koru Lifestylist reserves the right to pursue all available legal remedies against any individual or entity found to be infringing on its copyright.

In summary, Koru Lifestylist © 2024 holds exclusive rights to all the content produced by it, and any unauthorized use of such content will result in legal action.

To the Queen of Cosmic Eccentricity

In the kaleidoscope of my life, you, my dearest Mum, were the masterful artist, splashing vibrant hues of eccentricity onto the canvas of our sometimes boring existence. Your unique brand of craziness made my world infinitely more colorful.

In dedicating this book to you, I celebrate the whimsy you wove into my life, the wild dances of weirdness, and the echoes of laughter that reverberate with your signature brand of charm.

Thank you for sharing the brilliant, far-out force, weird force that you were.

With love and cosmic craziness,

Amanda xxx

Disclaimer: This Vibes Unveilled A groovy tarot guide to finding cool vibes, provides information on spiritual readings and interpretation, but it is not intended as a substitute for professional advice, diagnosis, or treatment. The information contained in this book is provided for educational and entertainment purposes only and is not meant to be taken as specific advice for individual circumstances. The author and publisher make no representations or warranties with respect to the accuracy or completeness of the contents of this book and specifically disclaim any implied warranties of merchantability or fitness for a particular purpose. The reader should always consult with a licensed professional for any specific concerns or questions. The author and publisher shall not be liable for any loss or damage caused or alleged to have been caused, directly or indirectly, by the information contained in this book. The use of this book is at the reader's sole risk

Why this book

Embark on a journey of cosmic discovery unlike any other with "Vibes Unveiled: A Groovy Tarot Guide to finding cool vibes." In a world filled with uncertainty and chaos, this revolutionary book offers a beacon of light, guiding you towards clarity, insight, and inner peace.

But why should you read this book? Because it's not just another tarot guide—it's a cosmic companion, a roadmap to unlocking the secrets of the universe and tapping into your own intuition. With its innovative approach to tarot reading, "Vibes Unveiled" empowers you to trust in the wisdom of the cosmos and embrace the magic that surrounds you every day... and you can take it with your anywhere so that the answers you seek are only a page flip away.

Whether you're a seasoned tarot enthusiast or a curious newcomer, this book has something to offer everyone. Through its pages, you'll learn to navigate life's twists and turns with grace and confidence, drawing inspiration from the vibrant energy of the cards and the groovy mantras that accompany them.

So why wait? Dive into "Vibes Unveiled" today and let the cosmic vibrations lead you on a journey of self-discovery, enlightenment, and transformation. It's time to unlock the mysteries of the universe and embrace the groovy magic that lies within.

Using the Book

Step 1: Groovy Book Vibes Cleanse

Hey there, cosmic book adventurer! Before diving into the cosmic wonders within these pages, let's vibe up and clear out any funky energies this book may have picked up along its journey to your hands. Step One and Two are like giving your book a cosmic spa day, and you only need to do it when things start feeling a bit clogged.

First things first, let's get grounded. Kick off your shoes, find yourself a chill spot, and connect those feet to Mother Earth. Feel that cosmic energy flowing through you? Yeah, you're grooving now.

Next, cradle your book in your non-dominant hand - that's your receiver hand, where all the magic flows in. Make a fist with your other hand and give the book a gentle tap. Bam! All those funky vibes are getting sent straight into the cosmic abyss.

Now, your book's feeling fresh and ready to vibe with your energy. Let's get groovy!

Step 2: Cosmic Book Blessings

Alright, groovy soul, it's time to crank up the cosmic vibes and infuse this book with your unique energy. Get comfy and start flipping through those pages, making sure to touch each one with your fingers, thumb, or hand. This is where the magic begins.

Now, hold the book in your dominant hand and bring it close to your heart center. Tune in to your inner vibes and think about the prayers or intentions you want to weave into the fabric of this book. Maybe you'll chant a little something like this:

"Hey there, cosmic peeps,
Let your vibes flow, guiding me with clarity and insight. Shower blessings on all who read these pages. Help me groove with my higher self, staying tuned in to the cosmic beat. Open my senses to hear, see, feel, and vibe with the sacred messages within. With reverence and gratitude, I seek your divine guidance. Peace-out, love, and cosmic hugs."

After this groovy ceremony, you might want to wrap your book in a silk scarf or stash it in a special bag to keep those good vibes flowing and ward off any unwanted energies. Groovy vibes only, baby!

Step 3: Groovy Reading Session

Alright, cosmic beings, it's time to tune into your inner vibes and perform a groovy reading. As you flip through the pages of the book, let your question float through your mind like a cool breeze on a summer day. Back and forth, forward and backward, until you feel that cosmic nudge to stop. Trust those vibes, baby!

Now, close those peepers and take a deep breath. Inhale the good vibes, exhale the stress, and count to three like you're counting down to a cosmic launch. Open your eyes and let your fingers do the talking as they land on the page that's perfectly meant for you in this moment.

Take your time, groovy cat, and read those words like you're sipping on a cosmic cocktail. Tune into your thoughts, your feelings, your senses—let them all groove together in harmony. And don't forget that mantra, baby! It's like your cosmic compass, keeping you grooving on the right path all day long. Peace-out baby!. Keep those vibes flowing!

Groovy Journal Pages

Hey there, cosmic explorer! Check it out: back of this book comes with its' very own journal spot! It's like your personal cosmic diary, where you can jot down your vibes, feelings, and what's up in your world while you're diving into the groove.

Don't forget to mark the date and scribble a little something-something—it's like leaving a foot print in your very own magical book of cosmic moments! So go ahead, let those vibes flow and make your mark on the cosmic canvas. Groove on, cosmic cat!

The Answers You Seek

Are Within

KING OF SWORDS

Cosmic strategist, the King of Swords conducts with clear vision. Groove in the cosmic symphony of intellect and leadership.

Mantra
"Wisdom's rule, cosmic school."

EIGHT OF PENTACLES

The craftsmanship groove, the Eight of Pentacles invites you to dive into skillful creation. Groove with dedication, let your cosmic talents shine.

Mantra
"Crafting dreams, in cosmic streams."

THE WORLD

Cosmic completion, The World spins with triumph. Groove with accomplishment, let the cosmic dance celebrate your journey.

Mantra
"Triumphant twirl, cosmic swirl."

ACE OF SWORDS

Cutting through the cosmic haze, the Ace of Swords is the groove of clarity, a psychedelic blade of insight. Ride the cosmic wave of truth and understanding.

Mantra
"Clarity's beat, truth's sweet."

TEN OF SWORDS

The cosmic crescendo, the Ten of Swords is the grand finale of challenges. Groove through the closure, rise from the cosmic ashes.

Mantra
"Rise above, cosmic love."

THE TOWER

Cosmic disruption, The Tower crumbles for rebirth. Groove through chaos, let the cosmic lightning spark renewal.

Mantra
"Chaos swirls, in cosmic twirl."

KNIGHT OF CUPS

The knight in shining emotions, the Knight of Cups is on a quest for love. Groove through the romantic adventure, let your heart be the guide.

Mantra
"Love's quest, heart's zest."

PAGE OF CUPS

A messenger of emotions, the Page of Cups is a cosmic text filled with creative vibes. Groove with inspiration, let the heart's poetry flow.

Mantra
"Heart's ink, emotions sync."

PAGE OF PENTACLES

A cosmic apprentice of practical magic, the Page of Pentacles brings vibes of learning and application. Groove with curiosity, let the cosmic scrolls of knowledge unfold.

Mantra
"Learn and grow, in cosmic flow."

QUEEN OF CUPS

The cosmic nurturer, the Queen of Cups flows with emotional abundance. Groove in the waters of compassion, let your heart's love be the potion.

Mantra
"Compassion reigns, in cosmic terrains."

THE DEVIL

Cosmic tempter, The Devil grooves with earthly desires. Dance with awareness, let the cosmic chains of temptation break.

Mantra
"Freedom's call, cosmic thrall."

FIVE OF PENTACLES

The cosmic winter of lack, the Five of Pentacles is a bluesy tune. Groove through financial chill, warmth lies in the heart's abundance.

Mantra
"Winter's blues, heart renews."

SEVEN OF SWORDS

Sneaky rhythms, the Seven of Swords dances with deception. Groove wisely, navigate the cosmic maze with cunning grace.

Mantra
"Sly moves, cosmic grooves."

FOUR OF SWORDS

Cosmic chill-out zone, the Four of Swords beckons you to recline in serenity. Groove in the quietude, recharge for the cosmic dance ahead.

Mantra
"Silent beat, cosmic retreat."

TEN OF CUPS

The cosmic finale, the Ten of Cups is a symphony of love and fulfillment. Groove in the harmony of family and joy.

Mantra
"Love's crescendo, cosmic innuendo."

THE HIGH PRIESTESS

Keeper of cosmic secrets, The High Priestess vibes with intuition. Groove with inner wisdom, let the cosmic mysteries unveil in the dance of the soul.

Mantra
"Intuition's flow, cosmic glow."

THE CHARIOT

Cosmic victory chariot, The Chariot races towards success. Groove with determination, let the cosmic wheels carry you to triumph.

Mantra
"Victory ride, cosmic stride."

TWO OF PENTACLES

Juggling the cosmic dance of balance, the Two of Pentacles invites you to groove with the ebb and flow of life's energies. Find your harmony in the jazzy juggle.

Mantra
"Balance beat, life's sweet feat."

Ace of Cups

Vibin' in the cosmic flow, the Ace of Cups is a psychedelic pool of love, dreams, and emotional bliss. Tune into the frequency of pure heart vibes, and let the love waves wash over your soul.

Mantra:
"Love's my groove, my heart's the move."

DEATH

Cosmic transformation, Death dances with rebirth. Groove through endings, let the cosmic phoenix rise from the ashes.

Mantra
"Endings blend, cosmic transcend."

NINE OF SWORDS

Midnight blues, the Nine of Swords is a cosmic symphony of anxiety. Groove through the dark tunes, find peace in the cosmic dawn.

Mantra
"Anxiety's fade, in the cosmic cascade."

TWO OF SWORDS

A cosmic crossroads, the Two of Swords invites you to find your groove in decisions. Blindfolded but not bound, trust the rhythm of inner balance.

Mantra
"Decisions flow, balance in tow."

SEVEN OF WANDS

The cosmic stand against adversity, the Seven of Wands is a defiant stance. Groove with courage, defend your cosmic groove.

Mantra
"Defiant stance, cosmic dance."

THE MAGICIAN

Cosmic spellcaster, The Magician grooves with mastery. Dance with the elements, manifest your desires with a groovy flick of the cosmic wand.

Mantra
"Elements align, in cosmic design."

SEVEN OF PENTACLES

Patience's cosmic rhythm, the Seven of Pentacles is the dance of waiting for the harvest. Groove with the cycles, trust in the cosmic yield.

Mantra
"Patience blooms, cosmic rooms."

SIX OF CUPS

Nostalgic vibes surround, the Six of Cups is a trip down memory lane. Embrace the retro joy, let the past groove in harmony with the present.

Mantra
"Memories flow, in the retro glow."

SIX OF WANDS

Victory's cosmic anthem, the Six of Wands is the triumph groove. Groove with confidence, let success be your dance partner.

Mantra
"Triumph's beat, cosmic feat."

FOUR OF WANDS

The cosmic celebration groove, the Four of Wands is a joyous dance of harmony. Groove with community vibes, celebrate love and achievement.

Mantra
"Harmony's dance, cosmic trance."

TEN OF PENTACLES

The cosmic legacy dance. The Ten of Pentacles is a generational symphony of abundance. Groove with family prosperity, let the cosmic wealth span generations.

Mantra
"Legacy's groove, abundance prove."

TEN OF WANDS

The cosmic burden groove, the Ten of Wands is a heavy but temporary load. Groove with determination, success lies beyond the cosmic climb.

Mantra
"Temporary load, cosmic road."

THREE OF PENTACLES

Teamwork's cosmic jam, the Three of Pentacles is the harmony of collaboration. Groove with fellow creators, let the collective energy amplify your success.

Mantra
"Collaborate, cosmic fate."

KING OF PENTACLES

The cosmic king of material mastery, the King of Pentacles leads with prosperity. Groove with abundance, let your cosmic empire flourish.

Mantra
"Prosperity's rule, cosmic school."

THE SUN

Radiant cosmic light, The Sun dazzles with joy. Dance with positivity, let the cosmic rays illuminate your path.

Mantra
"Joyful beams, cosmic dreams."

EIGHT OF WANDS

Rapid energy flow, the Eight of Wands is the cosmic messenger of swift change. Groove with the dynamic rhythm, let cosmic messages soar.

Mantra
"Swift transition, cosmic transmission."

NINE OF PENTACLES

Solo groove of luxury, the Nine of Pentacles celebrates self-sufficiency. Dance in the opulence of personal achievement, let independence be your melody.

Mantra
"Solo groove, cosmic move."

PAGE OF SWORDS

A cosmic messenger, the Page of Swords brings breezy vibes of intellect. Groove with curiosity, let your thoughts take flight.

Mantra
"Thoughts soar, in cosmic lore."

TEMPERANCE

Cosmic alchemy, Temperance blends harmonies. Dance with balance, let the cosmic elixir of life flow.

Mantra
"Harmony's brew, cosmic strew."

FOUR OF PENTACLES

Cosmic grip of stability, the Four of Pentacles asks you to groove with security without stifling flow. Find the balance between earthly stability and cosmic expansion.

Mantra
"Stability's hug, cosmic rug."

QUEEN OF WANDS

The cosmic queen of fiery charm, the Queen of Wands rules with charisma. Groove in the regal presence, let your cosmic energy shine.

Mantra
"Charisma's glow, cosmic show."

WHEEL OF FORTUNE

Cosmic wheel spins,
The Wheel of Fortune dances with fate. Groove with the cycles, let the cosmic winds of change carry you to destiny.

Mantra
"Cycles turn, in cosmic churn."

THE STAR

Cosmic wish upon a star, The Star beams with hope. Groove with optimism, let the cosmic energy guide you toward dreams.

Mantra
"Wishful gleam, cosmic dream."

QUEEN OF SWORDS

Intellectual queen, the Queen of Swords rules with clarity. Groove in the cosmic court of reason, let wisdom be your guide.

Mantra
"Clarity's reign, wisdom's gain."

PAGE OF WANDS

A cosmic messenger of inspiration, the Page of Wands brings vibes of enthusiasm. Groove with creativity, let the cosmic scrolls of possibility unfold.

Mantra
"Enthusiasm flows, cosmic prose."

ACE OF WANDS

Cosmic spark of creativity, the Ace of Wands is a psychedelic flame igniting passion. Groove with inspiration, let the cosmic fire burn bright.

Mantra
"Passion's blaze, cosmic daze."

THE HERMIT

Seeker of cosmic solitude, The Hermit vibes with introspection. Groove with inner wisdom, let the cosmic lantern illuminate the path within.

Mantra
"Solitude's song, cosmic gong."

EIGHT OF CUPS

The quest for higher vibes, the Eight of Cups is a cosmic journey. Groove away from the familiar, seek the beat of your soul's calling.

Mantra
"Higher realms, soul overwhelms."

FIVE OF SWORDS

Battle of vibes, the Five of Swords is a cosmic clash. Choose your battles wisely, groove away from unnecessary strife.

Mantra
"Vibes collide, in the cosmic tide."

SIX OF PENTACLES

The cosmic flow of generosity, the 6 of Pentacles invites you to share the abundance. Groove with charitable vibes, let the cosmic currency circulate.

Mantra
"Give and take, cosmic fate."

NINE OF WANDS

The cosmic warrior's stance, the Nine of Wands invites you to groove with resilience. Dance through challenges, let your cosmic armor be your shield.

Mantra
"Resilience's beat, cosmic feat."

KING OF CUPS

The emotional maestro, the King of Cups conducts the symphony of feelings. Groove in the regal flow of empathy and wisdom.

Mantra
"Emotional grace, in cosmic space."

EIGHT OF SWORDS

Illusion's dance, the Eight of Swords whispers in the cosmic winds. Groove out of mental binds, let liberation's beat set you free.

Mantra
"Mind's release, in the cosmic peace."

THREE OF WANDS

Expanding horizons, the Three of Wands is the cosmic vista of exploration. Groove with anticipation, let your ship of dreams sail into the cosmic expanse.

Mantra
"Horizons call, cosmic sprawl."

STRENGTH

Cosmic strength emanates, as the Strength card grooves with courage. Dance with inner power, let the cosmic lion's roar amplify your spirit.

Mantra
"Inner might, cosmic light."

THREE OF CUPS

Celebration vibes radiate, the Three of Cups is a cosmic party where joy flows freely. Dance in the groovy tapestry of friendship and shared laughter.

Mantra
"Joyful beats, cosmic treats, celebration in every street."

FIVE OF WANDS

The cosmic clash of energies, the Five of Wands is a spirited duel. Groove through the competition, find the harmony in diversity.

Mantra
"Diverse beats, cosmic feats."

QUEEN OF PENTACLES

Earthly queen of nurturing vibes, the Queen of Pentacles rules with warmth. Groove in the cosmic garden, let your care blossom.

Mantra
"Nurture's glow, in cosmic show."

SEVEN OF CUPS

Dreams take center stage, the Seven of Cups invites you to explore the fantastical realms of imagination. Groove through the possibilities, dance with your wildest dreams.

Mantra
"Dreamy haze, in the cosmic maze."

SIX OF SWORDS

Cosmic voyage, the Six of Swords sets sail for smoother shores. Groove through the transitional waves, trust the journey's cosmic course.

Mantra
"Smooth sail, cosmic trail."

JUDGEMENT

Cosmic call to rise, Judgement echoes with rebirth. Groove with redemption, let the cosmic gong sound your awakening.

Mantra
"Rise anew, cosmic view."

THE EMPRESS

Cosmic nurturer, The Empress is a groove of abundance. Dance with nature's rhythm, let the cosmic garden of life flourish.

Mantra
"Abundance blooms, in cosmic rooms."

KNIGHT OF PENTACLES

The steady knight of earthly vibes, the Knight of Pentacles rides with commitment. Groove with determination, let your cosmic journey be grounded and fruitful.

Mantra
"Steady pace, in cosmic grace."

JUSTICE

Cosmic scales balance, Justice grooves with fairness. Dance with integrity, let the cosmic equilibrium prevail.

Mantra
"Fairness flows, cosmic pose."

KNIGHT OF SWORDS

Cosmic speedster, the Knight of Swords races with ideas. Groove with the rapid flow, let your thoughts sprint towards dreams.

Mantra
"Swift mind, dreams unwind."

THE LOVERS

Cosmic union of hearts, The Lovers dance in harmony. Groove with love's rhythm, let the cosmic bond transcend earthly boundaries.

Mantra
"Love's embrace, cosmic grace."

THE HANGED MAN

Cosmic suspension, The Hanged Man vibes with surrender. Groove with acceptance, let the cosmic perspective shift your reality.

Mantra
"Surrender's sway, cosmic play."

THE MOON

Cosmic journey through the night, The Moon glows with mystery. Groove with intuition, let the cosmic tides guide your path.

Mantra
"Mystic beams, cosmic dreams."

THE EMPEROR

Ruler of cosmic order, The Emperor grooves with authority. Dance with discipline, let your cosmic kingdom prosper.

Mantra
"Authority's sway, cosmic array."

THE HEIROPHANT

Cosmic teacher, The Hierophant guides with wisdom. Groove with tradition, let the cosmic scrolls of knowledge unfold.

Mantra
"Wisdom's reign, cosmic gain."

KNIGHT OF WANDS

The adventurous knight, the Knight of Wands rides with passion. Groove with spontaneity, let your cosmic journey be filled with fire.
Mantra
"Passionate ride, cosmic guide."

TWO OF WANDS

The cosmic crossroads of potential, the Two of Wands invites you to groove with visionary vibes. Dance with possibilities, let your dreams set the stage.

Mantra
"Vision quest, cosmic zest."

THE FOOL

Cosmic journey's start, The Fool is a psychedelic leap into the unknown. Groove with spontaneity, let each step be a dance in the rhythm of trust.

Mantra
"Leap of faith, cosmic wraith."

TWO OF CUPS

A cosmic duet, the Two of Cups is a dance of souls, harmonizing in the rhythm of connection. Love vibes unite, creating a magical groove for two.

Mantra
"Two hearts, one groove, love's rhythm in every move."

NINE OF CUPS

The wish-fulfillment groove, the Nine of Cups is a cosmic DJ spinning your desires into reality. Dance with abundance, let your dreams rock the party.

Mantra
"Wishes flow, in the cosmic show."

FIVE OF CUPS

A temporary rain on the parade, the Five of Cups is a gentle reminder to ride the waves of emotion. Groove through the melancholy, find solace in the rhythm of acceptance.

Mantra
"Rainbow after rain, groovin' through the pain."

KING OF WANDS

The cosmic king of creative mastery, the King of Wands leads with inspiration. Groove with authority, let your cosmic kingdom flourish.

Mantra
"Inspiration's rule, cosmic cool."

ACE OF PENTACLES

The cosmic seed of abundance, the Ace of Pentacles sprouts into a groovy garden of prosperity. Dance in the earthly rhythms, let the material blessings flow.

Mantra
"Abundance blooms, in cosmic rooms."

FOUR OF CUPS

Chillin' in introspection, the Four of Cups invites you to vibe with your inner self. Find your groove within, but don't forget the groovy world around.

Mantra
"Inner peace, outer release, find the groove, let worries cease."

THREE OF SWORDS

Heartache's rhythm, the Three of Swords is a cosmic blues tune. Groove through the pain, let the healing melody soothe your soul.

Mantra
"Heal the hurt, in the cosmic flirt."

Vibes Unveiled

Cosmic Chronicles

Chillin' out ...

Chillin' out...

Chillin' out...

Chillin' out...

Chillin' out ...

Chillin' out...

Chillin' out ...

Chillin' out ...

Chillin' out...

Chillin' out...

Chillin' out...

Chillin' out...

Chillin' out ...

Chillin' out...

Chillin' out ...

Chillin' out ...

Chillin' out ...

Chillin' out ...

Chillin' out...

Chillin' out...

Chillin' out ...

Chillin' out ...

Chillin' out ...

Chillin' out...

Chillin' out ...

Chillin' out ...

Also by Amanda Clarke
More on the Bookshelves at
www.korupublishing.com